50+ Great Bathrooms by Architects

50+
Great Bathrooms
by Architects

Edited by Aisha Hasanovic

images
Publishing

First published in Australia in 2005 by
The Images Publishing Group Pty Ltd
ABN 89 059 734 431
6 Bastow Place, Mulgrave, Victoria, 3170, Australia
Telephone: +61 3 9561 5544 Facsimile: +61 3 9561 4860
books@images.com.au
www.imagespublishing.com

Copyright © The Images Publishing Group Pty Ltd 2005
The Images Publishing Group reference number: 637

National Library of Australia
Cataloguing-in-Publication data

50+ great bathrooms by architects.

Includes index.

ISBN 1 86470 144 7.

1. Bathrooms—Pictorial works. 2. Bathrooms—Design and construction.
747.78

Co-ordinating editor: Aisha Hasanovic

Designed by The Graphic Image Studio Pty Ltd, Mulgrave, 3170, Australia
www.tgis.com.au

Film by SC (Sang Choy) International Pte Ltd
Printed by Everbest Printing Co. Ltd, in Hong Kong/China

50+ Great Bathrooms by Architects is a book of ideas for those planning to renovate a bathroom, add an ensuite, or design a new home. It showcases main bathrooms, guest bathrooms, powder rooms and ensuites designed by many of the world's leading architects. Some houses feature static bathroom designs throughout the house, while others have used the opportunity to create a series of unique bathrooms within the same building.

Whether the designs are clean and simple or extravagant and luxurious, each responds to the desire for nurturing and pampering. Some bathroom designs factor a bather's privacy, while others feature floor-to-ceiling glass walls. The materials used range from tile and glass to recycled house materials and concrete.

Each individual bathroom is accompanied by a personal comment from the architect, whether it is a description of their favorite feature, or what they feel to be the most important element of the bathroom's design.

Whenever possible, floor plans have been included to indicate the position of the featured bathroom within the building. Sometimes there are simplified plans showing a basic bathroom layout, and many of the plans feature an approximate scale, in feet and meters, as well as a north arrow. The plans have been shaded so that the reader may identify the featured bathroom and other minor bathrooms within the building (see key below).

Aisha Hasanovic
Editor

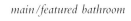 *main/featured bathroom*

 *other bathroom/s*

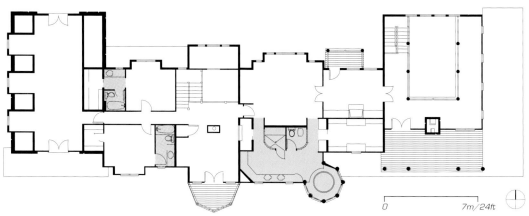

"The use of windows adds natural light to an otherwise dark space" DUBBE-MOULDER ARCHITECTS, PC

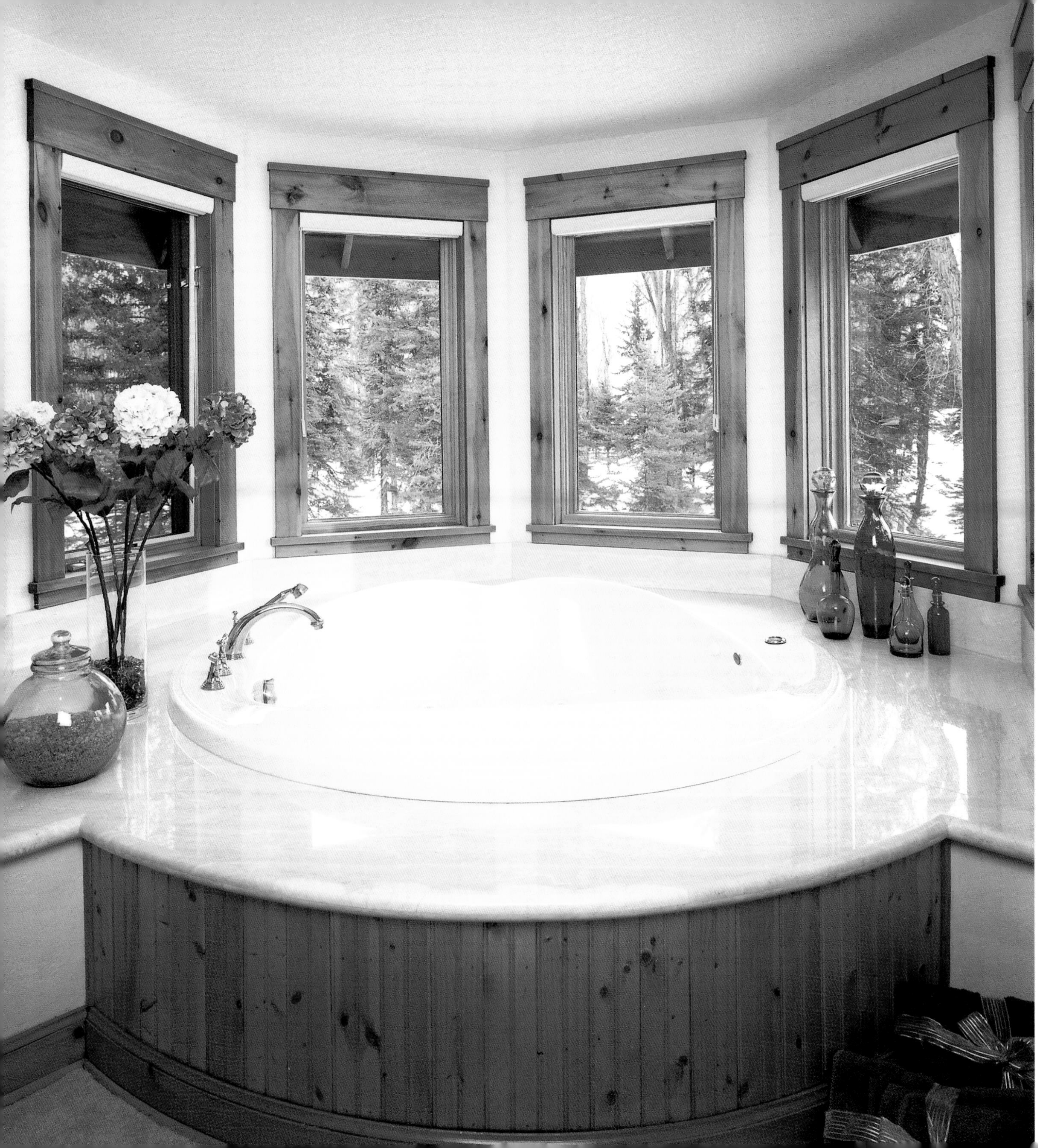

8

"Silver wall cladding is detailed to visually enlarge the small space" DAVID HICKS PTY LTD

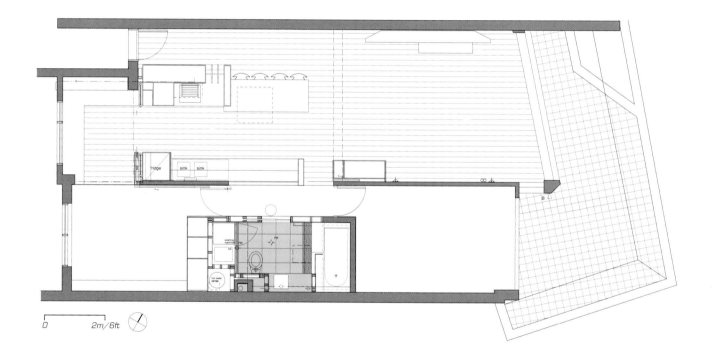

0   2m/6ft

"Only two materials have been used: Corian and limestone" STANIC HARDING

12

0   3m/10ft

"Clean lines result in a soothing atmosphere" CHO SLADE ARCHITECTURE

15

"Mirror extends space and appears to double the length of the window" STANIC HARDING

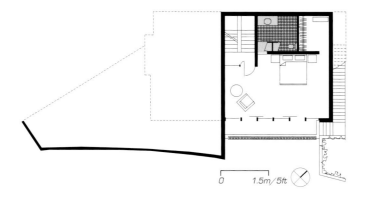

0   1.5m/5ft

"Combination of rough board form concrete, French limestone, and mosaic" STUDIO 0.10 ARCHITECTS

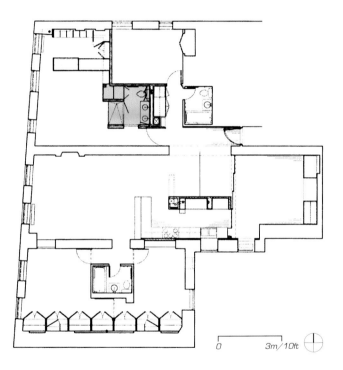

19

0   2m/6ft

"Mirrors extend space and reflect light into hallway via circular shower screen" STANIC HARDING

"Light reflects off glass, mirrors, and water" BOCHSLER & PARTNERS

"Bathroom becomes an extended living room with the use of glass for walls" OFIS ARHITEKTI

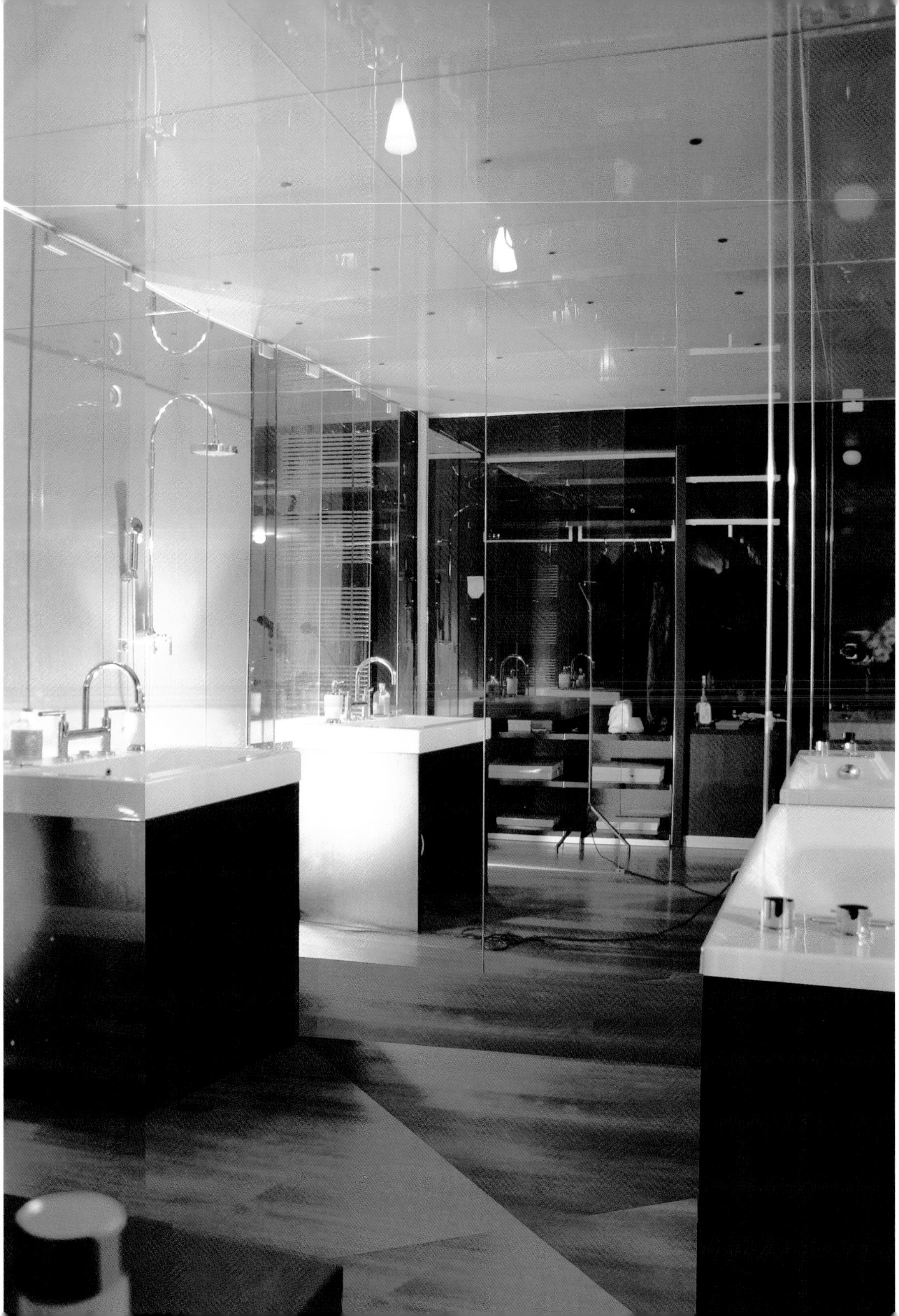

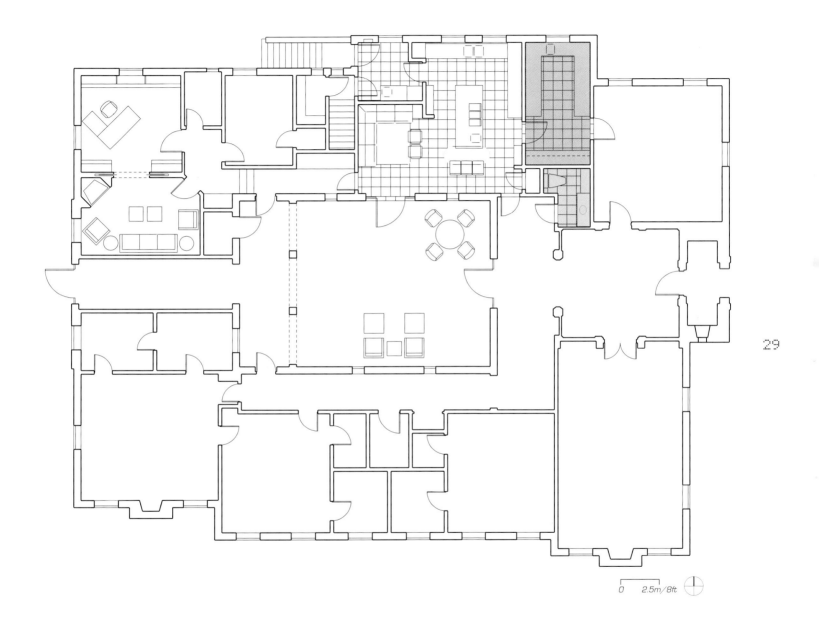

29

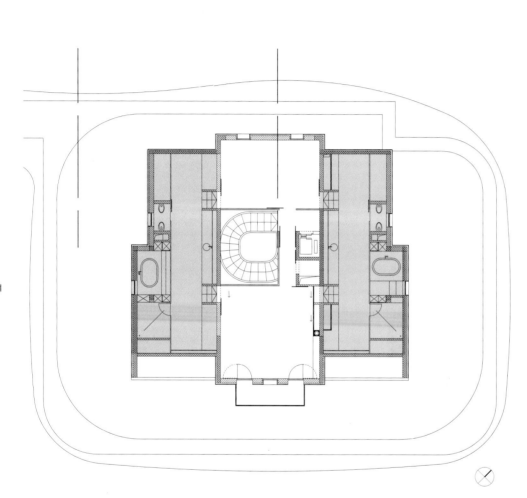

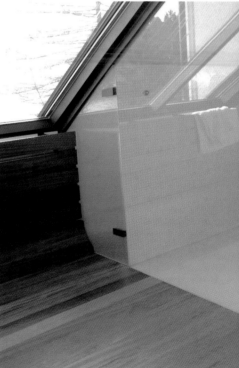

"Bath, shower, toilet, and washbasin are separate boxes on the left and right of the corridor...like on a train"
OFIS ARHITEKTI

"Glass mosaic tiles add richness to small spaces" STANIC HARDING

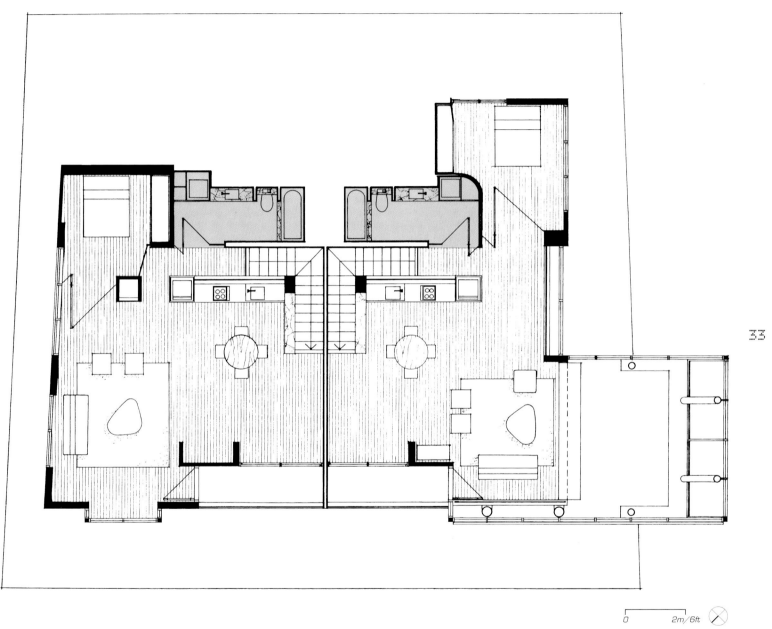

0   2m/6ft

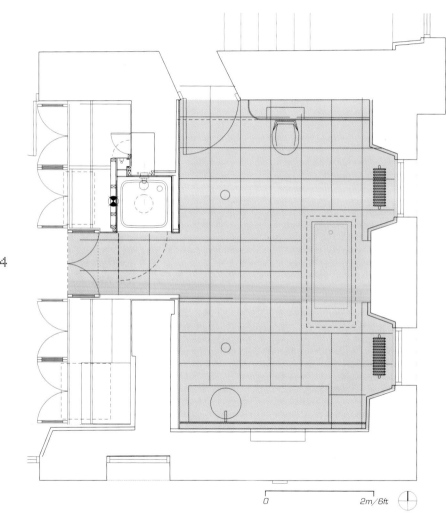

0   2m/6ft

"The bespoke recessed storage creates an uncluttered sanctuary" LEE BOYD

"Cool glass, warm stone, and rich wood impart an urban spa atmosphere" SHUBIN + DONALDSON ARCHITECTS

"The vanity hangs from the wall" MARK ENGLISH ARCHITECTS

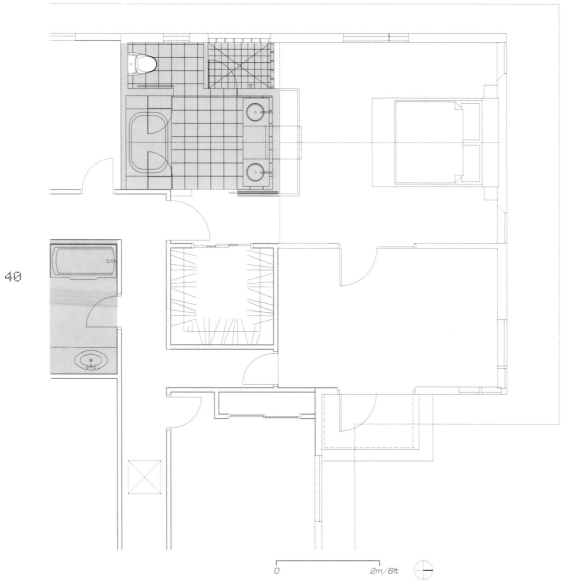

0   2m/6ft

"View of corridor through shower" AARDVARCHITECTURE

"Colored glass walls make internal spaces feel light" STANIC HARDING

0   2m/6ft

"Combination of natural materials and mirrors makes an interesting palette" DAVID HICKS PTY LTD

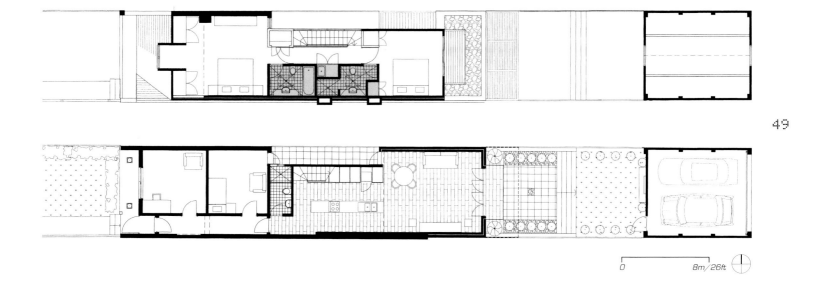

49

0   8m/26ft

"Skylight liberates walls and allows for full-height tiling" CULLEN FENG

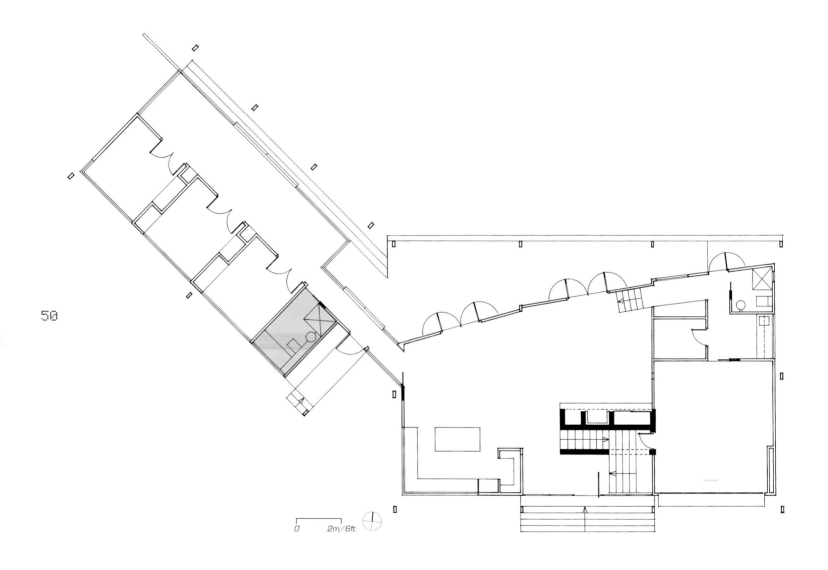

50

0   2m/6ft

"The fully-integrated sink captures all spills" CONNOR + SOLOMON

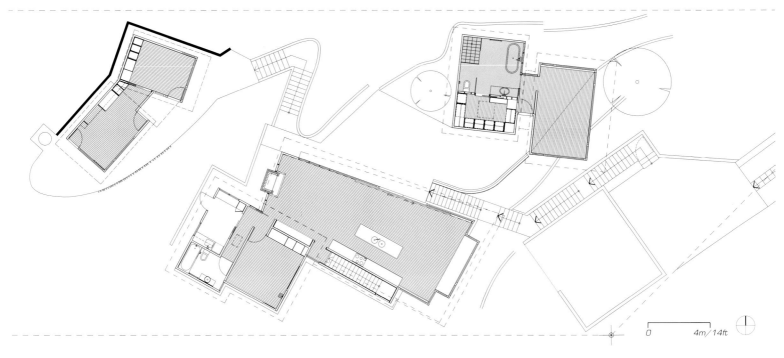

0   4m/14ft

"Light fills the spacious bathroom from all sides" DAWSON BROWN ARCHITECTURE

"Shower and toilet enclosures are fully glazed" CORBEN

0   2m/6ft

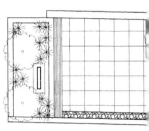

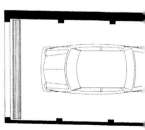

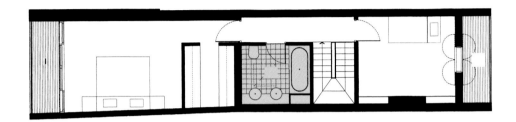

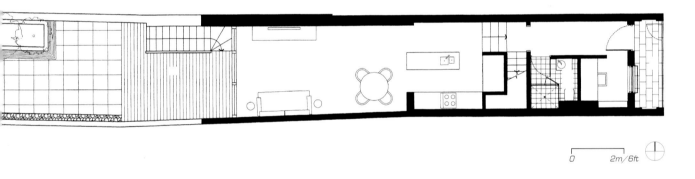

0   2m/6ft

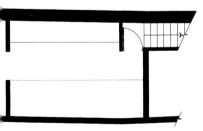

"Floating vanity increases perceived space" CULLEN FENG

"The continuation of master bedroom circulation and cabinetry organizes the shower room" RESOLUTION:4 ARCHITECTURE

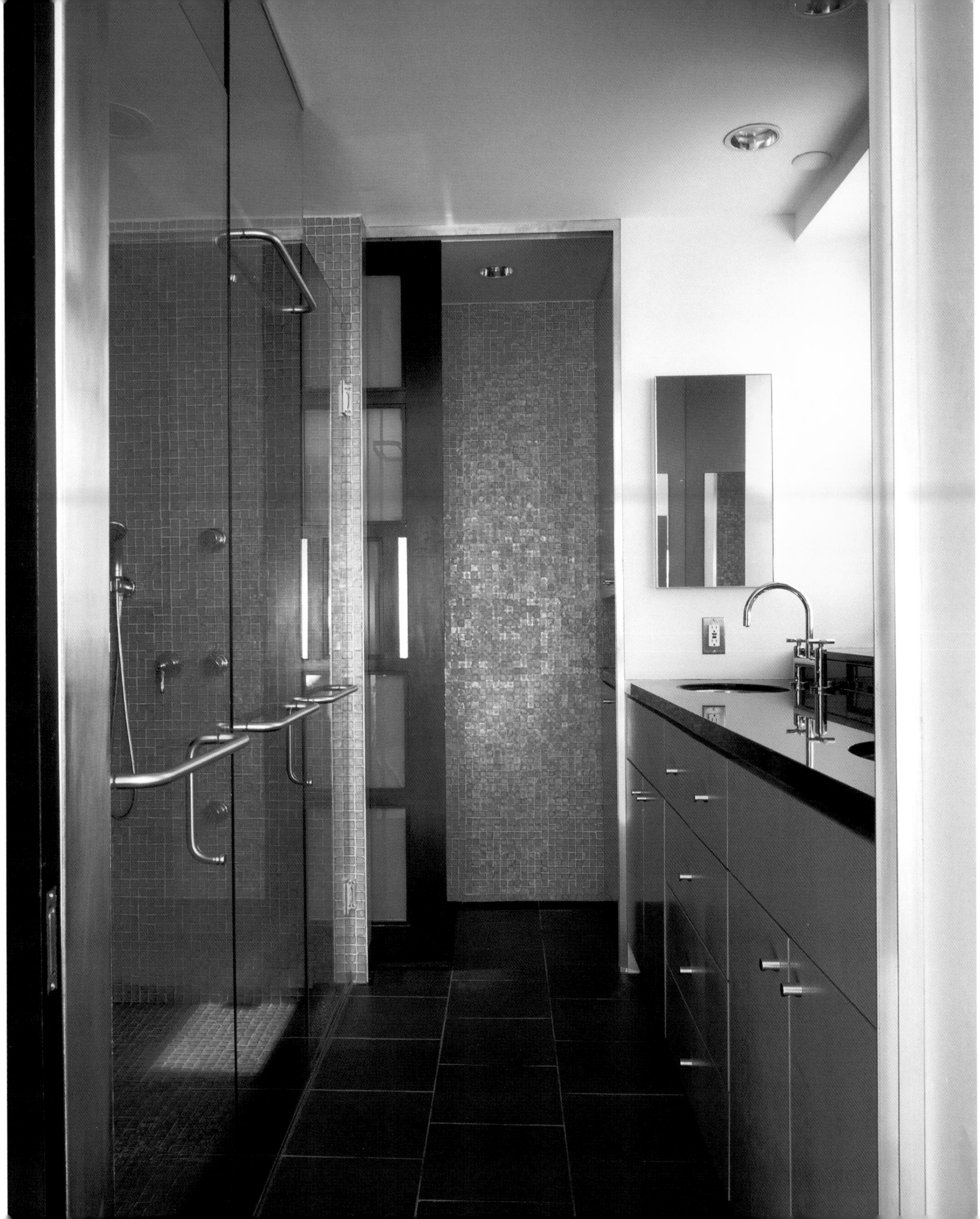

60

"Timber elements complement general bathroom finishes" STANIC HARDING

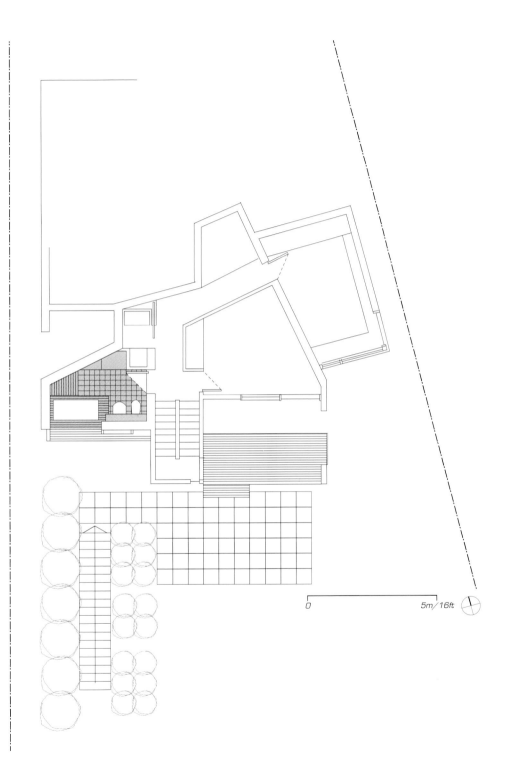

61

0   5m/16ft

"Light wood and textured marble ensure modern, yet warm feeling" MCINTOSH PORIS

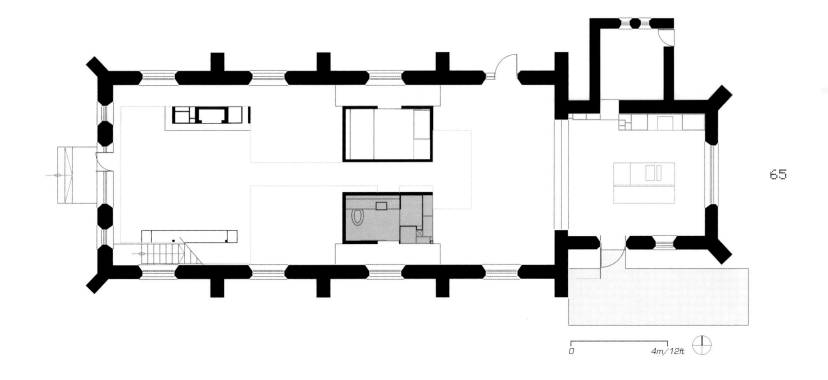

0   4m/12ft

"Mirrors reflect original stained-glass window and enlarge the space" MULTIPLICITY

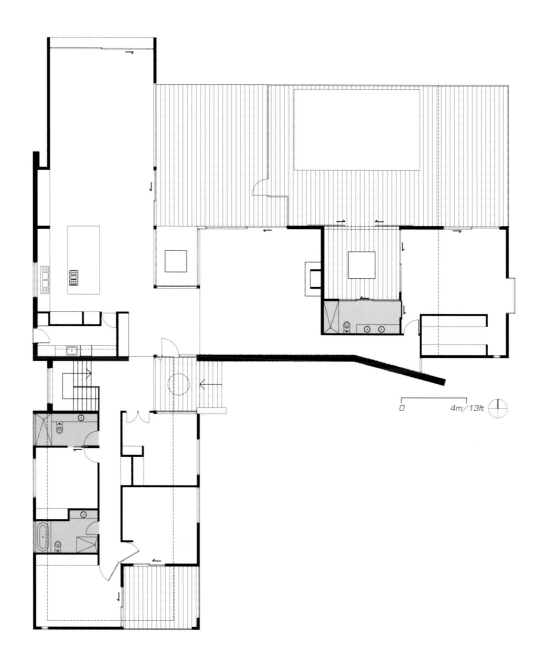

0   4m/13ft

"Materials and finishes are simple" BBP ARCHITECTS

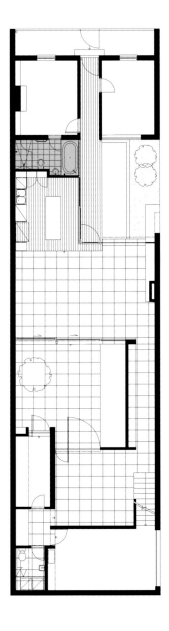

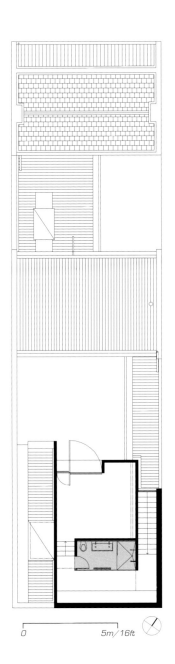

0   5m/16ft

"There is a strong physical or visual link with the outside" COY & YIONTIS

"Full-length stainless steel bench runs into the shower" SECCULL ARCHITECTS

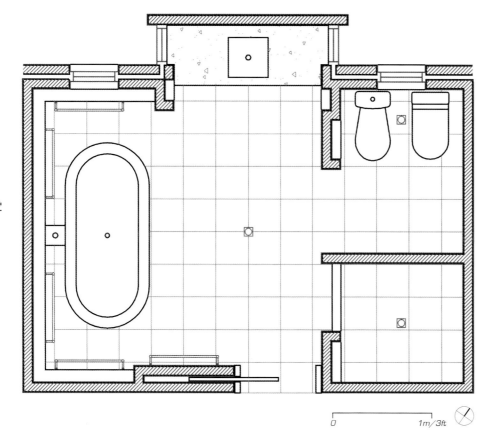

0   1m/3ft

"Subtle detailing, clean lines, and elegant bath create a sense of calm" CRAIG STEERE ARCHITECTS

"Shower is partly outside the building, giving a sensation of showering in the trees" STUTCHBURY PAPE

"Lit cubbyholes accommodate towels or other objects" SHUBIN + DONALDSON ARCHITECTS

"Central bathhouse allows views of the surrounding native plants" ELIZABETH & GABRIEL POOLE DESIGN COMPANY

"Sliding perforated screens provide a level of appropriate privacy" COL BANDY ARCHITECTS

"Creative use of one material: birch veneer plywood" ARCHIMANIA

"Stone and wood interact to create a sensuous tactility" CHA & INNERHOFER ARCHITECTURE + DESIGN

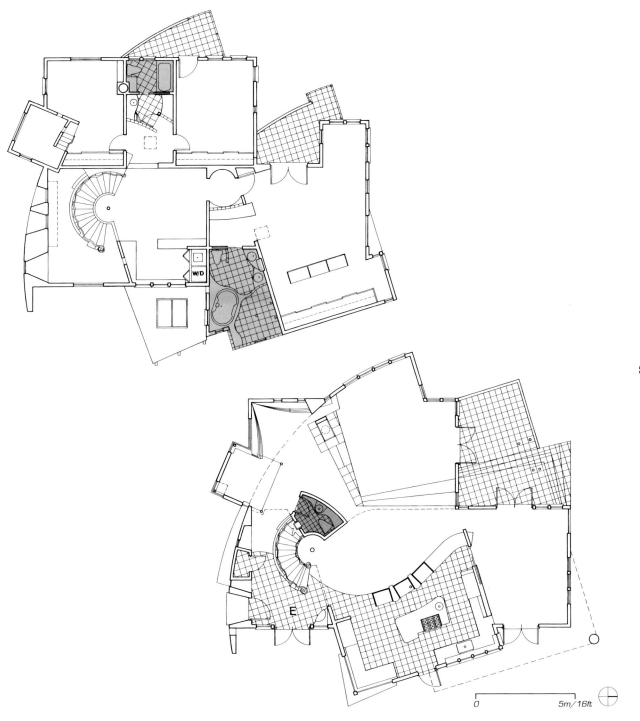

W/D

E

0   5m/16ft

"Sensual curving forms glisten with light and iridescent colors" HOUSE + HOUSE

"Fire-etched glass windows and doors allow light in, while maintaining privacy" SHUBIN + DONALDSON ARCHITECTS

"Backlit frosted-glass wall creates a greater sense of depth in a small room" SUPERKÜL INC ARCHITECT

"Areas are separated into wet and dry zones" BRIAN MEYERSON ARCHITECTS

"Elements float in a glazed lightwell" DALE JONES-EVANS PTY LTD ARCHITECTURE

"A soft palette of wood and concrete warms the sleek modern design" HOUSE + HOUSE

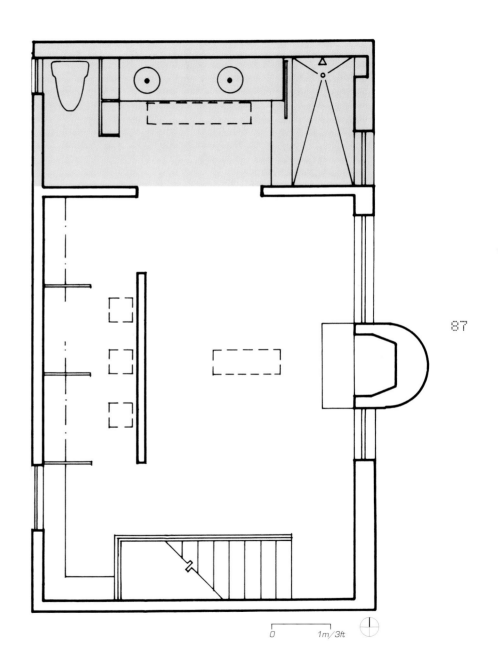

0   1m/3ft

88

"The bathroom's glass walls reflect light from the skylight" ENGELEN MOORE

"Light expansively links the bathroom to the outside" INTERLANDI MANTESSO ARCHITECTS

"The bath has glass-box bookends that contain a toilet and shower respectively" JACKSON CLEMENTS BURROWS ARCHITECTS

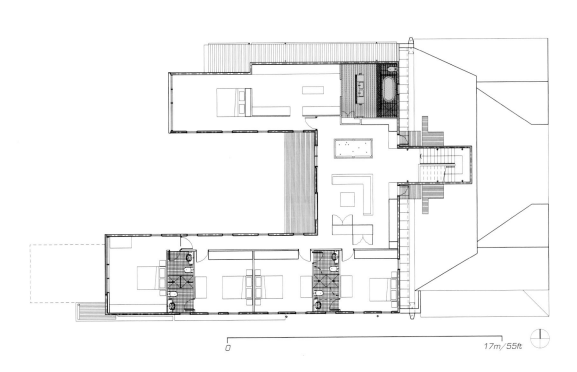

0   17m/55ft

"*Materials flow from one space to another for seamless visual connections*" OJMR

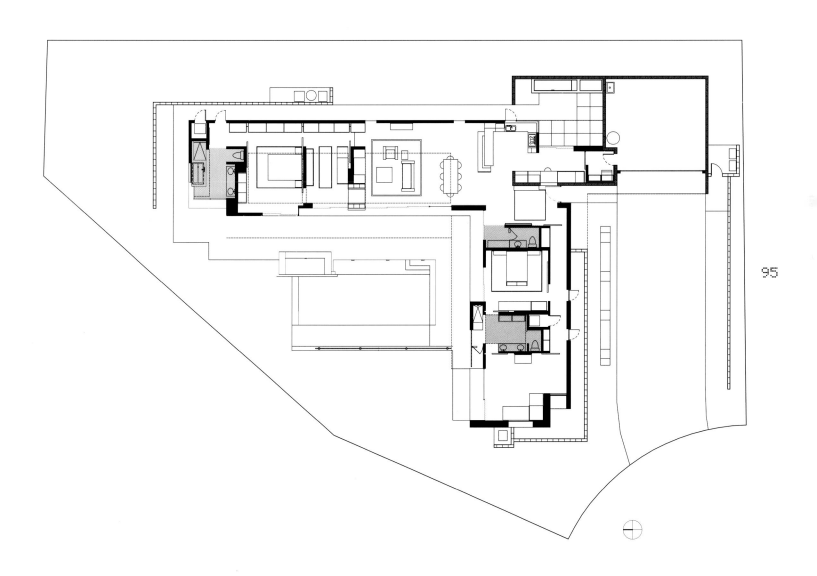

95

"The bather has a comfortable view of the outdoors" ELLIOTT + ASSOCIATES ARCHITECTS

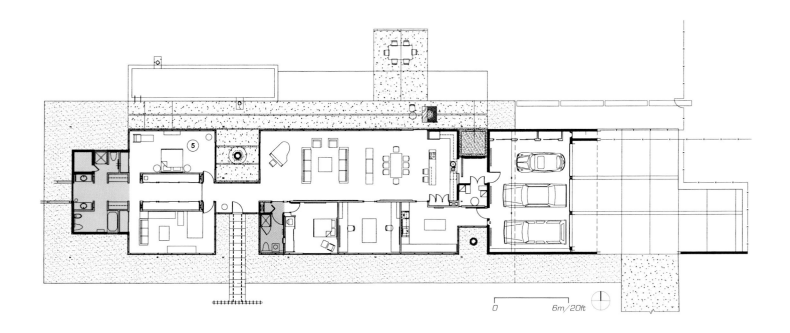

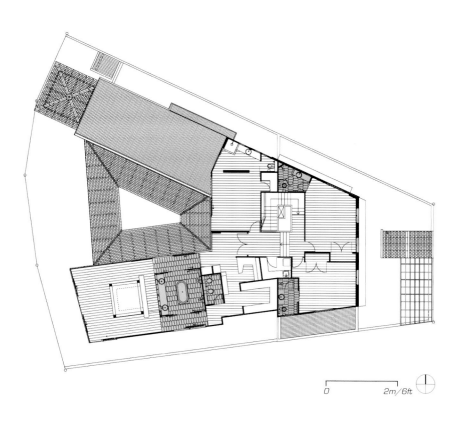

0   2m/6ft

"The materials are natural" BLIGH VOLLER NIELD PTY LTD

"Square basins complement the design" CCS ARCHITECTURE

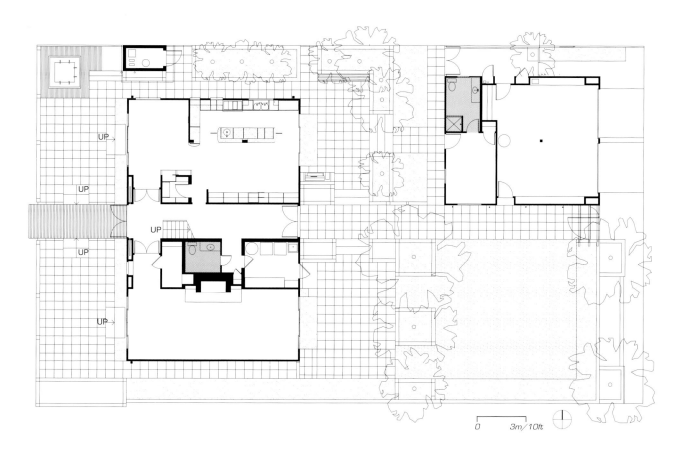

"A cubist composition in space and light" ALEXANDER GORLIN ARCHITECT

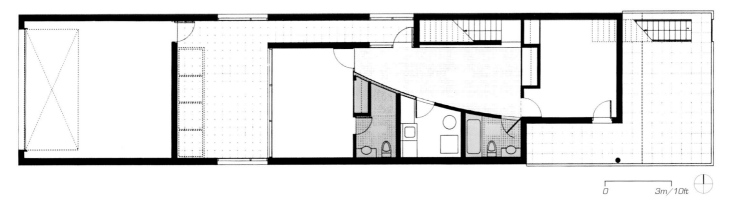

103

0   3m/10ft

"White marble slate creates a cool and calm setting" ALEXANDER GORLIN ARCHITECT

0   2m/6ft

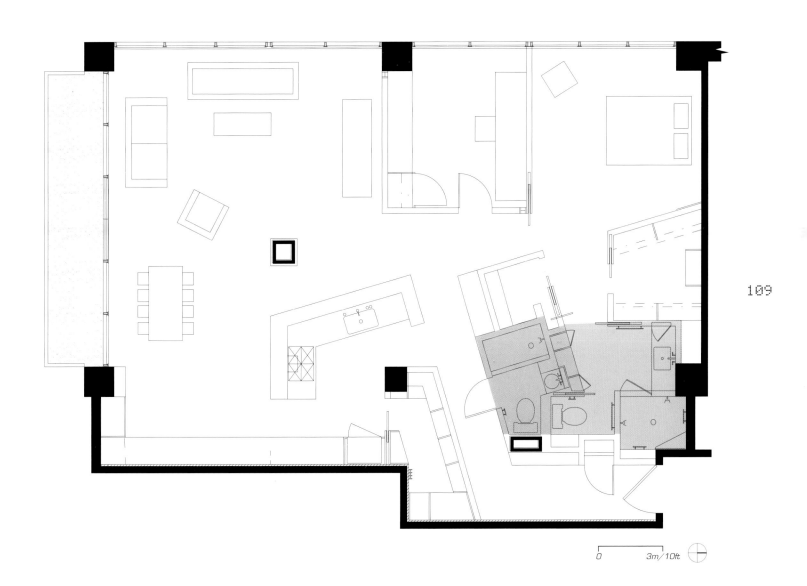

109

"A broken tile mural links rough geometry to a long brick vault" HOUSE + HOUSE

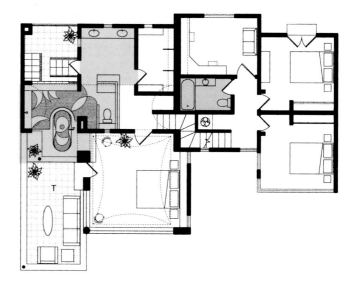

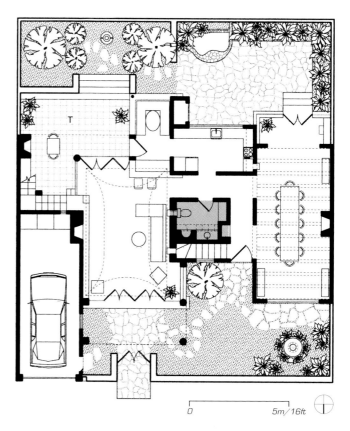

0   5m/16ft

0   7m/24ft

"A simple bathroom with rustic features" DUBBE-MOULDER ARCHITECTS, PC

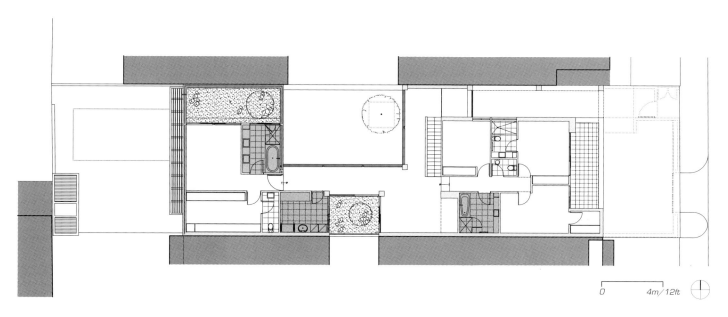

0   4m/12ft

"Framed view of partially hidden Magnolia" B.E. ARCHITECTURE

116

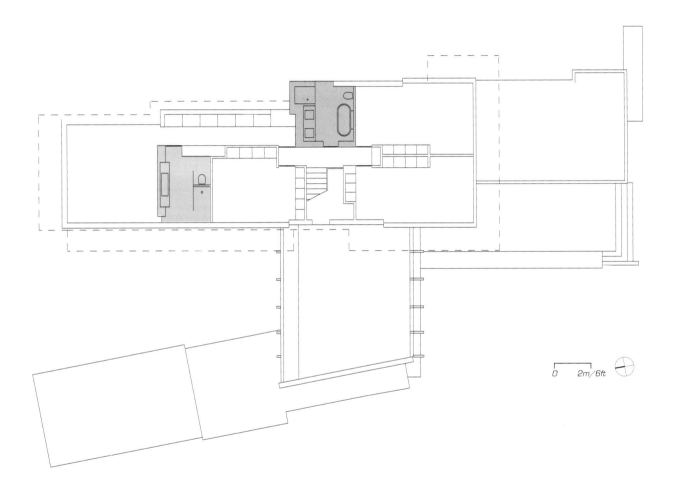

0   2m/6ft

"Space is intimate, with soft finishes and hidden utilities" MONCKTON FYFE

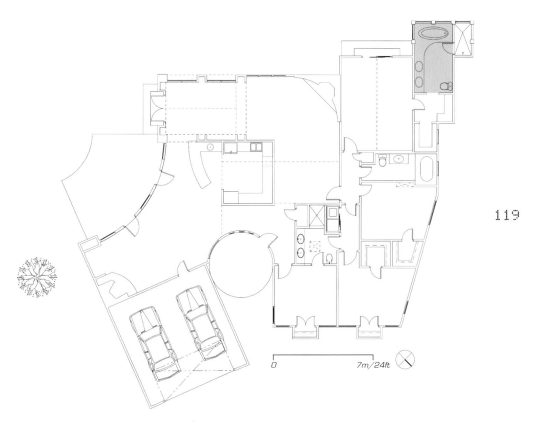

0   7m/24ft

"Designed around a unique curly-maple veneer" MARK ENGLISH ARCHITECTS

"Monochromatic use of materials and colors enhances the space" BBP ARCHITECTS

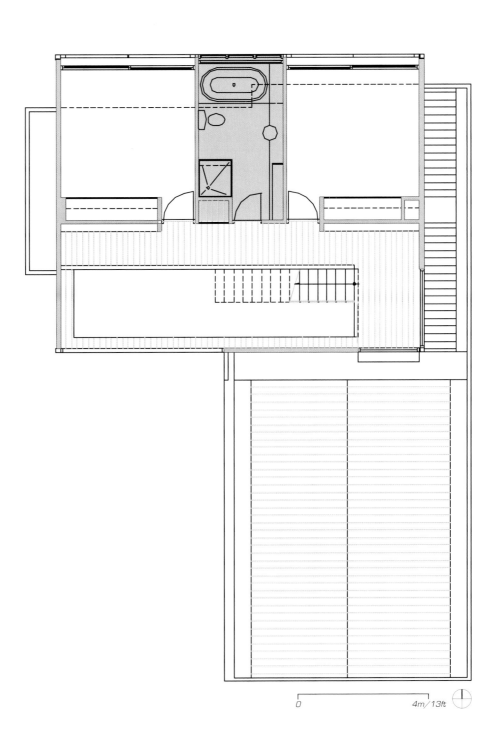

0   4m/13ft

"Reinvented veranda bathroom with mini-orb, timber, and recycled house components" JOHN MAINWARING & ASSOCIATES ARCHITECTS

"The use of marble makes for a sophisticated bathroom" OSKAR MIKAIL ARQUITETURA DE INTERIORS

Index of Architects

Index of Photographers

128